Goliath Is Falling!

Beating Big Business Online

Tom Carolan

Goliath Is Falling!!

Copyright © 2014 by Tom Carolan

All rights reserved. No part of this book may be reproduced or transmitted in any form or by any means without written permission of the author.

Special thanks to Scott Taylor, who helped name this book.

Foreword

There was a time when businesses just needed an occasional newspaper advertisement and a Yellow Pages listing to generate business. Maybe they would buy a space in the program for the local high school football team or give out pencils and pens with their name embossed on them for Halloween. The times were simple and gas was about a buck a gallon.

Those days are a memory. Welcome to the new age where the broadcast day never ends. Along with the 24-hour news cycles, entrepreneurs now have such a variety of options for marketing it's become overwhelming.

Marketing is a necessity… but can also make you feel like you're facing a giant you don't know quite how to conquer.

Like David who felled the giant with a simple slingshot and a smooth stone, this book can become your handful of rocks when it comes to conquering the world of marketing. Tom Carolan's aptly named *Goliath Is Falling!* will become your guide.

Wouldn't it be nice if we could all just put a web page and people would find us automatically, pumping in leads daily?

There's no chance of that right now. You need a list. You need traffic. You need a high converting offer. You need a nurturing sequence that moves prospects to clients.

All on autopilot.

All of this can be a full-time job – but the most profitable one in your company.

Tom's book walks you through what initially may feel like a marketing maze to you. After reading through this guide you will have much more confidence on how you want to tackle this aspect of business ownership. That marketing maze will soon become a clear, open playing field.

The Internet offers many opportunities for business owners and marketing representatives to generate new business leads. *Goliath is Falling!* will show you how to use what the Internet offers to your advantage, making your marketing effective and cost-efficient.

So much potential business is waiting for you and this book will show you the way. Grab a cup of coffee and let Tom Carolan show you how to conquer marketing.

Jeremiah Desmarais

Top 40 Marketers Under 40 in the US
23 Time Award Winning Marketing Executive, Speaker, Author
Cited authority on CNN.com, Worth, FOX News and NBC

Table of Contents

You Just Wanted to Do What You Do 1
Enter the Battlefield with a Plan 9
You Won't Like this Part of the Plan 19
Win Google as an Ally 33
The Never Ending Part of the Battle 49
Off-Site Reinforcements 57
Winning Your Neighborhood 79
Protecting Your Flank 89
Winning On the Go 99
Messages that Conquer 107
Wooing the Crowd 113
Map Out Your Plan 121
Glossary 127

You Just Wanted to Do What You Do

Congrats! You now have your own business, customers, staff, and the satisfaction of knowing you spend your days making money as you provide the products and services your customers want and need. The business is all yours (well, and the bank's or whoever you've got calling or mailing you to request monthly payments). And how terrific that you've accomplished your childhood dream of being someone who sells what they need, spending every day doing just what you LOVE to do.

OK. So maybe not.

In truth, if you could only time travel back to meet your young self, all optimistic and chomping at the bit to jump into this undertaking, you'd probably clobber yourself on the head for being crazy enough to imagine that you'd actually get to spend all day, every day doing what you love doing, and for thinking that would be enough to have a thriving business.

That younger version of you, bright-eyed and bushy-tailed, probably never dreamed of all the OTHER stuff you'd discover yourself doing day in and day out. The planning, the marketing, the sales, the organizing, the re-scheduling, the supply buying (how is it you manage to lose pens by the gross?), the accounts payable, the accounts receivable, the perpetual cycle of interviewing, hiring, training, firing, making payroll, bookkeeping, customer records management, insurance, continuing ed, paying taxes, contemplating buying new equipment, getting financing, taking deliveries, managing inventory, wading through manuals (no!), waiting for repairs… worn out yet?

Oh yes, and there's providing products and services for your customers. That's the original dream that set you on this path. How many years of school did you endure? Still paying those loans? How many hours of study, how many sleepless nights, how many gallons of coffee or green tea did you go through to learn all you had to learn? How much did you have to love the idea of your business in order to pull yourself through that endurance test? At some point, your love for it was enough to get you through. But, when you look at it now, it sure seems like you've got to do a whole lot of other stuff just to be able to do what you wanted to do in the first place.

The news gets even worse.

Just a couple of years ago, there was this big, thick, yellow book published every year that magically put some cash into your till. Prospective customers opened this book and found your business. They called. They showed up. They opened their wallets. You made money. The Yellow Pages... sure it cost you a fortune to advertise there, but it worked. Well, sort of. Sure, you grew to despise the sight of your representative, your wallet sweating every year when they came knocking, looking to renew your advertisement. You did it, mostly out of the certainty that if you didn't renew, your competitor sure would.

Now, you know it's not working. You practically feel like chasing your phone book rep out the door and through the parking lot, telling them not to bother coming back. That is, unless your customers fit particular die-hard telephone directory user demographics. Unless you're serving the phone book generation, your prospective customers do a direct deposit of new phone books into their recycling bin. In larger cities, they not only recycle one phone book, they probably send several back through the circle of life for trees. Advertising there is a gamble – what are the odds you choose the one particular phone book your new customers actually keep, and that they use it for anything other than a toddler booster seat, a doorstop, or for kindling in a fire pit?

If you're still advertising in the Yellow Pages, you're hoping the law of averages will work in your favor – that the more places you scatter your advertising dollars, the more likely some will stick, take root, and grow to become new business for you. This marketing plan is a rather expensive and frustrating way to bang your head on the wall.

You know your overall success relies heavily on how well you can get your phone ringing, your door swinging, and more customers buying. You need customers coming in today. You need them telling their friends. You need them coming back soon. You understand attending the odd networking event (and aren't they all?) or relying on word of mouth, or just being the best at what you do isn't going to be enough to keep your doors open.

You know you've got to get online. You've probably got a website. You might even like your website. Or, maybe it's terrible, a monstrosity built by your nephew, a former employee, a pre-made template, or some web guy who's gone out of business. You keep hearing how crucial it is to get your business online, to get to the top of Google, to develop an online presence, to use social media to attract and engage new customers, to mine the gold hidden in the hills of the Internet…

But really. What are the odds you've got the time, energy, or resources to take on one more (substantial) challenge connected to your business?

The thought makes you want to go looking for a sharp stick you could poke your eyes with, because that would be less painful.

Yes, I hear you.

That's why I'm giving you this book.

Providing products and services like you do in your business? That's your expertise. Well, my expertise is helping businesses like yours gain more customers through proven marketing strategies. I've invested time, cash, and sweat learning what works, exactly what does not work so well, and what's going to work most effectively for your kind of business. There's no way I'd even try to do what you do professionally for myself.

Haircuts? Dental cleanings? Electrical work? That would be insane. For sure it wouldn't be the best use of my time and energy learning how to do it, or trying to do it on my own. I wager that if you wrote and published a book on your specialty, breaking all the processes and best businesses down into workable action steps, translating all the lingo into plain English, I might be able to study long and hard enough to learn one thing: that I don't know enough to do it myself. I'd understand that getting a working knowledge would take more time, effort, and mental energy than I really want to give it – especially when I could just trust you to do it for me.

In a way, this is that book.

One way you'll benefit by giving it a fast read is that you'll be better able to avoid crooks. There are people out there who would like absolutely nothing better than taking your money and never lifting a finger to help you. Ideally this will give you enough knowledge to be able to spot and avoid them.

Or, perhaps you really DO crave total immersion in handling the marketing for your business on your own, and this will assist you as you learn exactly what's required to do it well. Maybe you've got nothing at all going on online for your business, and you're getting dragged kicking and screaming onto the web. The best way to protect yourself and your business is to learn the basics of what you need before you start writing checks to someone who promises you the world.

Or, possibly you're stuck in a deep, dark abyss where your website is concerned. It's ugly. It's nothing you're proud of. It's doing nothing for you. And your website developer is AWOL. It happens.

This book is intended to help you.

Relax. It's really not going to be that bad. In fact, today may mark a significant turning point in your business. By learning even a little bit about this topic, just enough that you can do something with what you know, you may be doing the one thing that keeps you from closing your doors (or wanting to) and finally getting your business headed in the right direction. The details you're about to skim through have assisted lots of businesses in seeing unprecedented growth – some doubling or tripling their customer base, even in the worst economy.

If your competitors have been mopping the floor with you, walking away with your customers, and driving you batty with how they seem to be everywhere you look, that's yesterday's news. Time for a new day. You can kiss your Yellow Pages rep goodbye forever, starting now. You're going to take your advertising in a whole new direction.

This quick read will leave you feeling smarter, more confident, and more optimistic than you've felt in a long, long time. You'll have clarity about what you need to do next, feel a flood of ideas and options buoying you up, and get the start of a whole tactical plan that'll work for bringing more customers your way. Best of all, you'll start seeing some sanity coming back into your business and life.

Enter the Battlefield with a Plan

You'd probably never start something big without a plan of action. Your plan doesn't need to be totally fleshed out to cover every possible detail or possibility, but without some planning, the road's going to be rough. The clearer your target, the more likely you are to hit it. With a well-defined plan, you give yourself every opportunity to enjoy the pleasure of watching it grow as new customers start coming your way.

More customers, better customers, customers coming out of the woodwork and sending their friends and family your way – that's the goal. Having as many customers as you can handle, all coming in automatically over and over again – how does that sound to you? What would a steady stream of new customers do for your business? How important is that to you?

How important is it to your prospective customers? Think about it from their perspective. Envision a restaurant you love. It serves the best (something) you've ever tasted. The service is so friendly you feel like you matter there. The place is beautifully decorated, perfect for an evening out, for meeting with friends. Going there is a highlight of your week, and you go there so regularly your friends know where to find you if you're not home. In fact, you like it so much that your friends have started asking if you're on the payroll, because you keep sending people there with a recommendation of your favorite dish. They raised the menu prices? You don't care. Neither did their other raving fans, who'd wait in line just for a table.

Does that mean this restaurant truly was the best place anyone ever ate a meal in the history of food? No. In fact, it probably benefited a little from getting good buzz. Someone ate there and liked it, and told two friends. And they told two friends. And so on, and so on, and so on.

Is it fair that we can't really quantify which businesses are truly the best? It's not really a matter of fairness. What makes one business great to a customer and another just okay is a matter of personal taste, assuming an equal level of skill, talent, quality, and selection in their products and services.

That's good news for your business.

See, even though you're probably on a never-ending pursuit of excellence, you don't have to be the hands-down best in order to serve your customers well and be successful. You're probably already the best in the minds of your loyal customers.

Becoming the best in the minds of your prospective customers is the goal behind your advertising and marketing. You want your business to be seen as the best possible option for people looking for somewhere to buy the products and services they want and need. They want to buy from the best, the expert. And that's you.

Why is this essential to understand?

People always prefer to be taken care of people they know, like, and trust. They want to find a business with an expert since time's short, resources can be tight, and frankly, who wants to spend time hunting around for someone who sells what they need they can trust?

Typically, people will assume you're an expert just because you're in business. The longer you're in business, and the more visible your business becomes, the more people will come to understand that you're an expert. Experts make more money.

The good news is, there's a lot you can do to boost people's perception of your business as THE place to go for the products and services you sell. It's not a matter of boasting, either. It's just a matter of helping people get exactly what they want and need.

How does this play out in your online marketing?

This is huge. It's the foundation of everything you need to do online for your business. You want it to be that anytime somebody goes looking online for someone who sells what they need in your local market, there you are. You want it so that almost everywhere they turn online, they find favorable reviews, map listings, directory site listings, news releases, short articles, videos, and more, all indicating that YOU are the go-to provider they've been looking for. If you do enough to promote your business (and provide value even to individuals who aren't yet your customers), you will win the game of online supremacy. Your rivals will have to run to catch up to you.

OK, so let's get to work. Let me offer you a general understanding of how this all plays out online.

Put yourself in your prospective customer's place. You sit at your computer and search to find... information on how to train your puppy.

What happens next?

- Chances are, you'll use Google (it's by far the most-used search engine, dwarfing all the others by a mile), although maybe you'll make use of Bing or Yahoo.
- You enter: puppy training (or something similar). This is called a keyword (or keyword phrase).
- You get a list of results (websites, videos, blogs, articles, and probably a few listings for trainers).

At the top of that list you'll probably have a few 'sponsored' entries. These are advertisements. They're at the top of the list because somebody spent good money for them to be there. The minute that advertiser stops paying for the ad, it disappears. It's the same with the list of results you see on the right of your screen.

As an aside, these ads are produced through a program called AdWords. It's a Pay Per Click (PPC) advertising model where you bid an amount you are willing to pay for each time someone clicks your ad. You only pay when they click. PPC can be a very valuable tool – but it can also be tricky. Unless you've got experience running a PPC campaign, or you have endless advertising and marketing funds, you might not wish to go that path on your own. It's easy to run up a big tab quite rapidly and not get much of a return on your advertising investment.

Anyway, once you scroll down past the ads, you get to what's called the organic listings. There are usually ten of these per page. These are web pages, articles, blog posts, and videos that Google deems relevant to your search.

This is crucial. Relevancy is vital to Google.

Here's why... if you went searching for ideas on training your pet and wound up with a list of sites that ranged from lasagna recipes to personal injury attorney videos to the advice on the best ways to sharpen a pencil, well, you'd most likely never ever make use of Google again. What does that mean to Google? Users equal money. Google frowns upon losing money. They are highly motivated to make sure that the search results they deliver are exactly what users are looking for.

With that in mind, when somebody goes looking online for someone who sells what they need, Google WANTS to include your business in those search results.

Problem is, Google's rather clever, but it does not know everything. And unless you've made an effort for Google to know details about your business, Google's not taking any chances in guessing what you do.

Back to our example. You've got a new puppy desperately in need of training. You're reviewing about 3.7 million results that Google recommended for you. Alright-- now it's time to read all them.

No?

The majority of online searchers stop scrolling when they reach the bottom of the first page. Some don't even go that far. They don't even scroll down. They just look at the top few results, and do another search.

Which items on the page are most likely to get clicked? The ones on the first page. The ones at the top of the first page, to be exact.

Not to jump ahead too far, but YOU WANT THOSE TOP SPOTS! In truth, the name of the game is getting as many front page listings as you can get, as high as you can get them. (Your competitor wants the same thing.)

Nobody understands precisely how Google identifies what's going to show up in those top spots. Internet marketers are constantly lamenting Google's business of changing the rules about what's on top of the list. It's like trying to hit a moving target. Nobody knows the exact recipe for getting to the top of the list – but an experienced marketer has some good ideas about what's working.

While we have no idea of the exact recipe, we have identified the best ways to make Google like a website enough to nudge it upward on the list. We know for certain what Google hates; and we know what Google says they want to see in a site they promote.

In a nutshell, Google dislikes being deceived. There's an entire specialty out there called "Black Hat SEO" which is tricky, bad guy kind of stuff. The entire objective of black hat is making Google like an Internet site it shouldn't like. Black hat tactics are constantly progressing, however in the end, the outcome is always the same. Ultimately Google identifies what the black hatter did, punishes the black hatter's website with invisibility, and makes a new policy that makes everything harder for everyone online – legitimate website owners included.

So, how do you make Google like your website?

You play fair. You offer real, important content. You don't play games.

Then, when somebody searches on Google for the products and services you offer, Google essentially thumbs through its huge Rolodex to find relevant results. If your site looks like a possibility, Google looks a little further, checking out what other websites say about your site. If everything seems to be in order, and Google's confident that your website is indeed relevant to what the search was all about, your site will appear in the search results list. It's almost like popularity contest, where there are votes cast all over the net for which sites are most relevant to any particular topic.

More good news. You can stuff the ballot box with votes for your site. Not only can you help ensure that your website gets listed toward the top of the results page, by doing so, you'll make it easier for prospective customers to discover you online (even if they have no idea you exist right now). They'll visit your site and be much more likely to call or visit, and they'll want to become your customer.

The rest of this book is going to lay out a strategy for you to achieve online dominance. It's a bit like playing chess. However, the object of the game here is to help new customers find the products and services they need and want... and to obtain them from you.

You Won't Like this Part of the Plan

Every project has that one gatekeeping kind of phase. You know, the bit where you're preparing, researching, analyzing, and pretty much chomping at the bit to get started – but constantly remembering that you've got to do this part first, or risk ruining that next part because you skimmed over the prep. It's like having to spackle, sand, tape, and prep a room before you paint.

It's not fun until you see results, but you've got to do this part to get those results.

I'd completely understand if you skipped this part of the project – you certainly wouldn't be alone in that. You'd get to dive right into the part that's a bit more fun (not much, but a bit). Of course, you wouldn't have any certainty at all that you were doing what you really needed to do – or that you were doing it right. It would be like climbing a big ladder up against a massive oak tree, and you'd be up on the hundredth rung before you realized… wrong tree.

What are we talking about? Keyword research, of course. And yes, it's even more tedious and dull than you're imagining right now. But it's necessary – unless you don't mind wasting time, money, and opportunity

Don't worry, we'll move fast, and it'll be over before you know it.

Keyword Research? What's That?
Keywords are what people type into Google (or any of the other search engines) when they need to find products, services, or information. It could be a single word, or a long phrase, or even a question.

Keyword research means figuring out exactly what those words are.

While it might seem obvious to you what someone should put into Google to find you or what you sell, you might be surprised.

You could hazard some pretty good guesses, but doing the research will yield a lot of terms you may never have considered.

Let's go back to your misbehaving dog as an example. Here's how people might go looking for help:

- train my dog
- dog needs training
- tips for dog training
- my dog barks too much
- stop dog barking
- puppy and dog training
- Siberian Husky training
- dogs hate UPS driver
- dogs barking help
- why dogs bark
- puppies need help with training
- teach my dog not to chew shoes
- …and thousands of other variations

Once you start researching, you'll discover some very strange search terms. They might be spelled incorrectly. They might use terms that are technically incorrect. They might even use terms that are completely outside your field – but somehow sound like they'd be relevant to what you do.

You just can't tell how your prospective customers will go looking for the products and services you sell. Guessing is guaranteed to yield results that miss the mark.

Here are four common errors businesses make when it comes to doing keyword research:

Error#1: They just don't do it.
Hopefully, you've already been convinced that this is a horrible idea.

Error #2: They steal from their competitors.
That sounds bad right off the bat. You might be surprised how often it happens, though. It's like the blind leading the blind. How do you know your competitor did a good job of keyword research? What if they did it wrong? What if they haven't done it in years? What if they got really bad advice about which keywords to go after?

This whole field has changed dramatically in just a few years, and what used to be perfectly sound advice back then would now virtually guarantee your website draws the ire of Google.

Yet it happens all the time. A business owner looks at the source code of a competitor's site, copies their keyword tags, and runs with them.

There are worse problems than the likelihood that these keywords aren't a good fit for your business. By copying your competitor, you've instantly increased how hard it will be to win – because now you're competing for the SAME keywords… and the other guy had them first.

Worse still, you're competing for dominance on keywords that you don't even know are any good, anyway. Even if you manage to achieve higher rankings on the search engine results page than your competitor, these may not be the keywords anyone's really using who'd become your customer.

Error #3: They don't USE their keywords.
This happens a lot. A business owner gets a list of keywords and then doesn't know what to do with it. The list gets filed somewhere safe, and never sees the light of day again.

Keyword research isn't fun. The only thing that makes it worthwhile is applying what you discover. Without implementation, you just suffered through a tedious project for nothing.

Error #4: They forget to do it again.
Once is never enough. Keyword research is one of those tasks you have to do fairly regularly – although not daily or weekly, thank goodness!

Why? People might grow more aware of some of the products and services you sell. The more they know, the more specific they are in how they search. This is good news, because a more specific search is usually done by someone who's on the brink of buying.

For example, who do you think is more likely to buy very soon?

- Someone who searches for "car parts"
- Someone who searches for a super-duper OEM Relay Fuel Cut-off Gold Wing Magna Sabre fuel injector

If a more specific term becomes more frequently used by prospective buyers, you'll want to use it in your online marketing.

There's another reason you shouldn't do your keyword research once and call it a day. Doing it right takes time. You can't do it all in one shot. You'll do better by following a pattern of researching, then implementing, then as you make progress with getting traffic from some of those words, go back and do more research and repeat the process.

An additional reason for making keyword research a regular part of your online marketing process is that within your field, there are likely to be significant changes in the coming years. Maybe new products and services will become popular. Maybe you'll get advanced training. Maybe some products or services will develop a bad reputation (it happens!). You might take on a new product line, invest in new equipment, or start using some new technology. Your online marketing will need to reflect these changes.

So, how is keyword research done?

I wish I could tell you all you had to do was punch a few buttons, and out would pop a nice list of solid keywords… but it's not true. It's not quick. It's not easy.

However, there are a couple of tools that might work for you. (Professional marketing firms have access to some very expensive, thorough, and complicated tools – but they really wouldn't be suitable for a business owner who doesn't have the time to devote to going through the learning curve needed to work with them.) Some business owners decide to outsource their keyword research to a firm that can handle it for them, which at least would give higher quality research results.

The tools of most interest to you would fall into two camps – those you pay for, and those that are free.

Free: Google's Keyword Planner
This tool has undergone a lot of changes over the years, and is only accessible to registered AdWords accounts. You don't have to run ads, but you have to have an account. The research results focus on how you'll fare in competing with other paid advertisers – even if you're not paying for ads. It's still useful information because you don't want to go after keywords everyone's going after… or that nobody's going after (there may be a good reason).

You can do your research with this tool two different ways. One is by entering 'seed' or starter keywords into the search field; the other is by entering your existing website into the website field and allowing Google to guess what your site is about. Obviously if you're just starting to work on your site, or if it hasn't been optimized for keywords (a good likelihood for most businesses) Google may have a hard time coming up with good keyword suggestions just by analyzing your site.

By entering some seed keywords into the tool, you can get keyword suggestions Google deems relevant in relation to those words. Some of them may surprise you. Some may be misspelled (your searchers don't always know how to spell your products and services, and sometimes they search without typing carefully). Some may include an 'incorrect' term (again, your searchers may not appreciate the subtleties of the semantics and jargon in your field). They may also include search terms that are way more specific – or vague – than you would anticipate. For example, a search for air conditioning repair may actually come up as someone looking for a specific manufacturer's part number. Google's suggestions are generally pretty good – but you may find some that are completely off-topic.

The primary information you'll be able to gather from this tool is how many people searched for various keywords within the past month. There are tutorials on YouTube and in Google itself that will help you learn how to gather and interpret keyword data. There are ways you can do your research that will yield more or less valuable information.

Because the tool is intended for advertisers, you'll see some metrics that reference how competitive different keywords are based on how much advertisers are paying for their ads to show up for those keywords.

Market Samurai
This is a paid keyword research tool that won't break the bank. It's far more robust, providing not only keyword suggestions, but multiple filters you can use to make sure the suggestions you get are as applicable as possible. It uses Google's data for some of its reports.

In addition to keyword suggestions and search volume statistics, this tool makes it easy to identify your top ten online competitors for any particular keyword. You'll be able to gather some valuable information about their online marketing efforts and what it will take to surpass them for your best keywords.

You can also track your website's progress in domination for different keywords. This means you can see at a glance how well your site is ranking on the three major search engines (Google, Bing, and Yahoo) for your keywords. You'll see what page your site is showing up on, whether you're gaining or losing ground, how many pages on your site are being indexed (meaning the search engine has noticed that page and is checking back periodically to see whether anything's changed on that page), and how many backlinks (we'll get into that later) point toward your website.

There are many other functions and features in Market Samurai, and the publisher offers dozens of video tutorials that make learning this software possible. You'll also find tutorials on YouTube which may be helpful.

Whatever tool you choose to do your keyword research, be prepared to spend several hours learning how to use the tool, then several more doing your research. It's not a fun task, but investing the time and effort needed to do it right will pay off.

What Qualifies as a Good Keyword?
The specific criteria for keyword evaluation varies depending on the market, the niche, and the marketer. Essentially, a good keyword is like low-hanging fruit on a tree… easy to reach and pick. There should be enough search volume (people using that keyword in Google) to make pursuing it worthwhile – and not so much competition that you'll have a hard time dominating for that keyword.

In some niches, like car insurance as an example, keywords are exceptionally competitive. Advertisers may pay $25 and up to have their Pay Per Click ads show up when a searcher inputs certain keywords. Competing for those keywords is going to be tough, and require you to publish an enormous amount of content – or buy very expensive advertising – in order to get traffic. On the other hand, other niches are up against far less aggressive competitors, and are likely to see good results with less of an investment.

You need to find your niche's sweet spot – keywords that have a reasonably high search volume and that are not being pursued by competitors with deeper pockets than you. Once you've gathered some of these low-hanging fruit keywords, go after them as you continue looking for more that are similarly attractive.

If you aim for keywords that are too competitive, it will take much longer to make progress as far as your Google placement. You'll be in competition with businesses that may have been going for those keywords for years, businesses that may have much deeper pockets or a dedicated Internet marketing department. If you aim for keywords that are "too easy" they most likely won't have enough search volume to make your efforts pay off.

Maybe an example will help…

Some keywords have virtually no valuable search volume. In most cases, your own name would qualify for this example. Type it into Google, and you should come up at the top of the list of results – unless you have a very common name or the same name as a celebrity.

That might seem like a good keyword, because you're already dominating the search results list. However, odds are there aren't a whole lot of people searching for what you sell by using your name. There's not much competition, but there's also not much search volume.

If you type in a broad term related to your niche, you'll get a ton of search volume, but the competition will be too stiff to make pursuing that keyword's traffic a viable option.

You want to find keywords that your prospective customers will use to look for the products and services you offer – even when they don't know your name or your company's name. You may have even better luck going after keywords that also feature your geographic location, because most likely your customers will be located nearby.

Start compiling a list of your best keywords and save them. A spreadsheet is ideal for this because you can keep track of which keywords you are pursuing, what you're doing to get traffic from them, and how you're succeeding in your efforts.

It's a good idea to prioritize your list – and color coding makes your job even easier so you can tell at a glance which keywords you're going after first. Once you make progress with your first targets, keep moving down the list.

In the next chapter, we'll start looking at what you'll need to do with the keywords you've identified as winners for your business.

Win Google as an Ally

It's time for some acronyms. The primary term you need to know, and have probably heard thrown around for a couple of years is SEO – Search Engine Optimization. This section's going to cover what's needed SEO-wise as you promote your website.

What Does SEO Mean?
SEO is all about how you make a website irresistible to search engines like Google, making it obvious that your website is truly relevant to what people are looking for as they search for your products and services. Google looks at every bit and piece of your website and forms an opinion – either loving it or hating it.

In this way, Google is a lot like a stray cat – except it's one you want to keep hanging around. If you set Google treats out, it'll keep returning for more. If you make Google like your site, becoming confident that it's full of high-quality content searchers will like, not only will Google keep coming back for more – it'll also send real live people your way when they go looking for information like what you've published. Trick, tease, or taunt Google, and it will scratch your eyes out.

Like it or not, Google is the king of today's online world.

So, what makes for a good website that Google approves and sends traffic to? Of course, we can only surmise from what we do know about their secret checklist, but some elements are a sure bet. The essential premise behind interpreting Google's preferences for one site over another is that Google's not happy about sending searchers to sites that they don't like. When a searcher lands on a site like that, the next action they take is going somewhere else immediately. It could be because the first site wasn't even remotely what the searcher expected to see, or just that they didn't like they layout or feel of the site. Google prefers websites that keep visitors there a while, looking at multiple pages, reading content, and delving into the information they find because it's valuable.

One of the most important goals with your website is building your online presence and credibility. Visitors to your website need to get the idea that you are an expert, and that they're reading what a leading authority has to say.

A little aside here...

Remember how we compared Google to a stray cat? You've got to realize that Google lives to prowl around, checking out what's new online, what's changed, what's available. We refer to what their system uses to gather this information as 'bots' or 'spiders' – and what they do as 'indexing' or 'crawling' the web. One goal is to get Google to index your site quickly and to keep coming back, to get it to notice and like as many pages on your site as possible.

Think of each page on your website as one more way you try to woo Google, supplying it with good content so it determines that your site is, in fact, an authority site it can trust will delight most visitors that end up there.

What Every Page Needs
Each page on your site will have a different emphasis content-wise, but there are certain technical elements you'll need to work in to have a fully optimized site.

Headline

Every single page on your website needs an attention-grabbing headline that's benefit-driven. Most sites don't have that at all – they'll have something like one of these:

- Thanks for Visiting Our Website
- ABC Company Has Been in Business 25 Years
- Forget the Rest, Buy the Best (whatever it is they're selling)

Yawn.

Instead, in just a couple of lines, you want to communicate the biggest benefit someone gets from doing business with you rather than anyone else. You probably already know what that is – in business training, they call it your unique selling proposition. One easy way to zero in on this is to identify the biggest pain, fear, or hassle your customers no longer have to deal with because they're doing business with you. People are highly motivated to escape suffering – so if you can show them how they'll do that by dealing with you, you're on the right track. Put yourself in your customer's shoes. Create a website viewed through the eyes of the customer.

Not only do you need a compelling headline – it also needs to feature your best keyword. This makes it easy for people to know this site is where they'll find what they need. It also helps Google's bots understand exactly what your website is all about.

Keywords

In the "old days" web developers would just dump every keyword under the sun into your site – even if it wasn't quite relevant, and Google was okay with that. Now, Google has gotten smart, and part of its algorithm involves using something called latent semantic indexing (basically does that language make sense and flow naturally, or does it look like someone went crazy stuffing keywords in where they don't belong, harping on the same words over and over?).

Best business is to choose one keyword (this could be a single word or a whole phrase) to highlight per page. Of course, you'll naturally use other relevant terms in the course of writing your website copy – and that's perfect. But you need to have a single focus for each page.

Your keyword needs to show up in certain places:
- Your headline
- Sub-headlines
- First sentence of the body of your text

- In bullet points
- In your call to action (we'll cover that shortly)
- In your anchor text (we'll cover this, too)
- In your list-building box (coming up, too)

There's a term "keyword density" you'll need to pay attention to, also. Again, in the old days, the rule was the higher the density, the better. Not so anymore. You can calculate keyword density by doing a simple calculation:

- Count how many times you use your keyword in your text.
- Check the page's total word count.
- Divide the page's word count into the number of times you used the keyword.

The sweet spot is 1-2% density. So, for every 100 words of text, your keyword appears 1-2 times. More than that, and you'll need to be a super-skilled copywriter to make it sound halfway decent. Much more than that, and Google will hate your page and consider it to be spammy (stuffed keywords, garbage, not credible... bad!).

Word Count
While the goal of your content is to say what you need to say, it matters how long you take to say it. The length of your content matters as Google evaluates the

authoritativeness of your site. Even though your visitors (most of them, anyway) don't want to read through lots of text, if the text is too short, Google won't like your pages. Nobody knows the sweet spot Google looks for regarding word count on a page, but you don't want to go lower than about 350 words per page. Make sure to break your text up to be pleasant to read. Do this by using subheadlines, bullet points, short paragraphs, and white space.

Formatting

People have exceptionally limited attention spans – especially when they're online. Very few people will sit down and read every word on your site. Instead, visitors skim, scan, and scroll their way through website content, trying to pick out the bits of information they need most.

If you write your content so that it appears as one long block of text, that's a sure way to have your visitors click off of your site and onto your competitor's. Nobody wants to read that way online.

Instead, break your content into short paragraphs. Bold subheadlines work to keep your visitors reading your content. Bullet points are a good thing, too – but don't over-do them.

White space is important. Your page should look good, easy to read, welcoming, and user-friendly. Studies show that dark fonts on a light background is the most readable combination. The opposite might look attractive, but it's better to stick with what's proven to be most effective.

Include photos and videos in your website – people always like to 'see' as well as read about how you can help them.

Call to Action
So you got someone to visit your website. They've been reading up on the products and services you offer. They now know what they need to know before they will feel comfortable buying from you. But what will they do then? Not a thing, unless you tell them what they should do next. It sounds silly that they won't figure that out on their own, but in most cases you have to actually spell out the next step.

Include a call to action on every single website page. Tell your visitors what to do next. This could be having them call you for an appointment, get a free consultation, visit your business, click to get a free report, complete a form, or something else. Many businesses even include an appointment request form or the ability for a customer to schedule appointments online from the website for added convenience.

Anchor Text

This is a little techy, but it's important. Imagine a big hairy a spider on a web. (No screaming!) There are two main types of web – the pieces that go around in circles, and the pieces that go from the outer edges to the center.

That's a good model for your website. You want to move visitors to your site through your site so they'll get what they need and get into your sales funnel. You also want to create a cohesive site that people can navigate easily.

This is where anchor text comes in. It's a tactic called internal linking. Most of what you'll read about for creating website traffic refers to external linking – also crucial, but different from this.

Anchor text is the words someone actually clicks to get somewhere else online. They're attached to code that takes the visitor to another page or section of your website. It can be helpful to work the next page's primary keyword into the text your visitor clicks to reach that page.

Here's an example. On an attorney's website, let's say one page's keyword is "trusts and estates". Another page might include a hyperlink to a completely different page about trusts and estates that might look like this:

Have questions about <u>trusts and estates</u>?

Your website visitor would click the words "trusts and estates" to reach that page.

Doing this wrong is really common. How many times have you seen text that says "click here" to get to another page? Do this and you'll entirely miss a great SEO opportunity. Google notices what kinds of words are used in your anchor text, because it further cements its impression of what your site is all about.

Building Your List of Prospects
This topic will be covered more in depth later, but we'll start the discussion here because of how important it is to make sure this appears on every page of your website.

You'll hear online marketers refer to their "list". Here's what that means...

Let's say a prospect lands on your website, reads a bit about your business, even maybe gets excited that they've found you. But then something happens. They get distracted. They go do something else – anything else – besides calling you or following whatever else you've issued as a call to action.

What are the odds they'll remember where they found you?

Not high.
You now have a hot prospect you can't reach. They're gone – probably forever. You certainly can't market to someone who's gone.

If you build a list, you end up with a group of people who want what you're offering, who want to hear from you, who want to do business with you eventually. These will be some hot, self-qualified prospects.

You will need an email service like Aweber or Constant Contact (there are tons more out there, too). These are pretty easy to use, and not very expensive. It's important to use a service like this rather than trying to send hundreds of emails from your own email account. That's a good way to get your account closed. These services specialize in getting your emails out while complying with all the regulations connected to email marketing.

With these services, you'll set up a list, create a form, and get a bit of code to add to your website to create a subscription box. This is just a little area of your site where you'll offer something (usually a free report, a video, something like that) to people who provide their name and email address. For best results, make sure this subscription box shows up on every page on your website. People often don't take action the first time they see something – but if it's on all of your pages, they may join your list – and then you can stay in contact with them until they ask you to stop.

Contact Information
Your business's phone number should be prominent on your page – in your header is an ideal spot. Don't make people work hard to find that information. Your business' physical address is the same – make it easy to find.

Credibility Bits
Remember that your visitors have a single question running through their minds as they visit your site – is this the business I've been looking for? Nobody wants to do business with someone who's shady, someone they're not sure is a good solution, someone other people have had bad experiences with in the past.

You can help your perceived credibility by adding the following to your website:

- Your picture – or a picture of your team
- Logos from associations or groups you belong to (anything from your specialty or your local community)
- Logos from any product lines you carry
- Testimonials or reviews from your happy customers

Which Pages Does Your Website Need?

At a bare minimum, you need these pages:

Home

About Us

Products or Services

Contact Us

Articles (or Blog)

Privacy

Home

This page is all about first impressions. It may be the trickiest to get right, because you've only got about three seconds to convince your visitor that they're in the right place to find what they're looking for, that you are the one they want to do business with. Google also pays close attention to this page.

About Us
This is a very important page for establishing your expertise and credibility. On this page, you want to communicate why you're qualified to deliver on the promises you make in your unique selling proposition. Remember, your visitors are trying to decide whether they know, like, and trust you. This page, more than any other is your opportunity to make that happen for your visitors.

Products and/or Services
This page is often overlooked because the content may seem too obvious to you as the business owner. For example, if you're a chiropractor, you know you offer spinal exams, adjustments, X-rays, nutritional and fitness products, and more. However, you need to spell this out on your products and services page. It's a great opportunity to highlight anything special about how you deliver these services, too. This page is especially important for showing Google what you do.

Contact Us
Even with your phone number displayed prominently on your website, you still need to have a Contact page. On that page, include your address, phone, even a map to your location. Do NOT include your email address there because you're guaranteed to get swamped with a million

spam emails then. Instead, you can include a contact form your visitors can complete to contact you.

Articles (or Blog)

OK, this one's really a blog, but many people have a wrong impression of what that means. This is not the "here's what I ate for breakfast" kind of blog. It's really just an easy way to publish frequently, building the credibility and size of your website while you build a connection with your prospective and current customers.

Having a blog or articles page on your site is so important that we'll give it the whole next chapter.

The Never Ending Part of the Battle

Your blog is pretty much a Google magnet if you do it the right way. With a great blog, some marketers get more traffic than their counterparts who pay for traffic with those sponsored ads in Google. Blogs are updated frequently, which means Google's bots come back frequently – this further cements Google's impression of your website as being an authority in your specialty.

Of course, if you do it wrong, nothing good will come from it.

So, let's dig into how to blog well. If you master this for your business, you'll have a huge head start over your competitors.

What Is a Blog?

There are lots of ways to build a website – but one of the most powerful is to have it built using the WordPress platform. Google loves sites built this way. Your site will still look like a 'normal' website – but it'll also feature a quick and easy way to publish blog posts (articles, really!). So, you'll have the usual pages for your website, and then also an articles page which features all of your blog posts. You can categorize them, add 'tags' which help visitors find posts that give them the information they're looking for at the time, you can add images and videos, you can even allow for discussion on the content.

Who Needs a Blog?

You.

OK, a little longer explanation. Every business needs to have a blog. It's that important.

What's Involved in Blogging?

Blogs are a lot like articles. (We'll cover articles in the next chapter.) They're more fun to write, though, because unlike writing articles to publish in article directories (again, wait for the next chapter!), you've got complete editorial control. You can write like you speak, talk about whatever you want as often as you want, any way you want. You can be opinionated, somewhat promotional, controversial – however you want to cover your topic, it's all good.

Some particulars:
- Your posts can vary wildly in length, but generally you want to go 250-500 words.
- You'll need a good, compelling title that'll spark your visitors' curiosity and make them eager to read what you wrote.
- You'll also need to write a 1-2 sentence teaser – kind of a cross between a summary and a mini sales piece giving a visitor a reason to read the post.
- You'll need to have a keyword for each post and use it in your title, teaser, first sentence, as an ALT tag for any image you use, to tag your post, and possibly as a category for your post.
- Remember to write using short paragraphs, headlines, subheads, bullets, and white space.
- Always have a call to action at the end of your blog post. What do you want readers to do next?
- You can also create internal links to other blog posts and sections of your website that are relevant to the topic. Be sure to use a keyword as the anchor text.

How Often Do I Need to Blog?

You may not like the answer. Every day would be ideal. No way do you have time to do that, though. So, 3-5 times a week would be really good. Once a week is okay. Once a month is better than nothing.

The neat thing is that with most blog setups, you can write a bunch of blog posts at once and then set them to publish whenever you want them to. So you could write an entire week's worth or a month's worth of posts and then set the publishing date in the future at whatever interval you want. That way you can kind of set it and forget it – and still get all the benefits.

Whatever frequency you choose, it's important to be consistent. Don't be overly ambitious and think you'll blog every day – unless you really get into it, you won't. Most businesses can handle blogging three times a week. The reason consistency is important is that your blog is a great way to train Google to come back and check for new content – and at the same time, you can give your readers an idea of how frequently they should come back expecting new content.

What Should I Blog About?

You'll like this – there are some very easy ways to get ideas. If you think about the prospect of writing 3-5 times a week for your blog from now on, it's more than a little overwhelming. How many ideas could you possibly get for topics to write on?

One way to get ideas is to visit sites where people ask questions about your topic. Yahoo Answers is a great example. You can search on something relevant to your specialty and most likely you'll see hundreds of questions asked and answered by real people.

Compile a list of these questions, and keep checking back, and you'll have a pretty-near, never ending list of topics to cover. Keep the ideas in question form, because it's always easier to answer a question than to just write off the top of your head. Plus, if someone enters that question into Google (it happens all the time!), your post has a great shot at coming up in the search engine results.

Another way to get ideas is to ask yourself some questions about different services, ideas, products, and businesses within your specialty and blog the answers:

- What is it?
- Why is it important?
- What benefit is there to doing/buying this?
- What if I don't take action?
- How do I do it?

- What if I do it wrong?
- Who could do this for me?
- How often does it need doing?
- How can I learn how to do it right?
- Where can readers find resources or tools that would help?

Yet another way to get an endless stream of ideas is to set Google Alerts for your topic. You'll need a Google account for this (it's free). All you have to do is Google "Google Alerts" and you'll come to a page that walks you through the process. You'll just enter different terms (your keywords are a great start!) you want Google to watch for you. You'll provide an email address where the Alerts will go – and you can specify whether you want to get them daily, weekly, or immediately when Google finds them. You can see anytime that keyword appears in the news, on a website, or in someone's blog. Then just go through your inbox and look for Alerts that spark ideas for your blog.

One thing you never want to do, though, is to copy someone else's article or blog post into your blog. Google has ways of knowing who published it first – and you won't get credit for the post at all if Google thinks you copied rather than writing it yourself. In some cases, businesses have done this hundreds of times a day – the end result was a Google smack that landed their sites useless.

Most businesses find they just don't have the time to write their own blog posts. It's probably one of the most-outsourced projects out there. There are websites out there where you can find a ghostwriter – many online marketing professionals offer blogging services to their clients as well.

If you decide you do want to tackle blogging for your business, there are also many courses and books available that can teach you other tips, tricks, and tactics for using your blog to make money in addition to your regular income stream from your business. There are bloggers out there who make very good money just from their blogs.

This should be enough to get you started, though.

Now that we've covered all the basics you need for making your website powerful and effective – and helping Google to fall in love with it – it's time to look at the other half of the equation: off-site SEO.

Off-Site Reinforcements

Once your website's in good shape, SEO-friendly, and built for power, you need to start carving out your place on the Internet. It's all about links: creating as many very high-quality links on high-quality sites as possible... all pointing to your site as an authority. We refer to all this "pointing" as backlinks.

In the early days, there was a push for begging, borrowing, and buying links from other sites. Google caught on.

Lately, the trend has been to follow the throw a bunch of spaghetti on the wall and see if it sticks model. Google caught on.

Turns out the best way to get links is the old-fashioned way... to earn them.

It does get a little overwhelming here – so get ready, and remember you don't have to do all of this yourself – or to do it all at once. Online marketers often have tools and other resources that help to make these tasks much easier – so they actually get done! The learning curve and price tag on some of these resources are steep, so they may not make sense for most business owners to get for themselves, though.

The general principle behind all you'll need to do to promote your site all over the Internet is that you want to be known in all the right places, constantly growing the perception of your site as being an authority in your specialty.

If you think of it, on a massive scale, there are sites you consider authority sites – sites where you know for sure you'll get the information, products, or services you need. For example, for books, you'd go to Amazon. For music, iTunes. For an online auction, eBay. For info on medical symptoms or conditions, WebMD. For info on pretty much anything else, Wikipedia or About.com.

Not that these sites are the best, or have 100% accurate information or the lowest prices – it's just that they've built their online presence to the point where they're pretty much unavoidable online.

This, on a smaller scale, is the goal for you with your off-site SEO work. You want it to be that when a potential customer does a search on your keywords, you show up all over the place – the clear and obvious leader and expert.

Now, if you had to rely on other website owners to notice your site, like it, want to help promote you, and actually do something about it, you'd be sunk. It'll never happen.

The good news is all of the tasks we're about to cover are fully within your control. You're at nobody's mercy, really. It's a LOT of work to do it all, but it can be done.

Ready?

Submission to Search Engines

Even though we talk pretty much exclusively about Google, there are hundreds of other search engines. Most of them have tiny user bases compared with Google, but there are some diehards who still prefer to use them. We won't even list them here, because most of them are about an inch away from extinction. However, you can do a quick Google search and find them.

Most of these search engines have a tab somewhere that allows you to submit your site. Some of them have a review process your site will have to go through before it's approved. Some of them require you to categorize your site, and to provide information about your business.

You can Google "submit website to search engines" and you'll find links you can use to submit your site. Be sure to submit it to the big three: Google, Bing, and Yahoo. But also submit it to everything else you can find, as long as it's not a search engine dedicated to a topic that's completely irrelevant to your specialty.

You'll need to do this periodically. It's tedious. It's pretty labor intensive without tools. But it's important, and if you do it frequently enough, it'll become a pretty easy and straightforward process.

Submission to Local Listings
The bigger search engines now have local listing opportunities as well, and you'll need to get into those listings. We'll cover Google's local listings in a later

chapter, but for now, just know you'll need to do that – and to get into every other local listing you can.

An easy way to get started with that is to Google: local listings. You'll find a long list of places to submit your website.

Again, you'll need to have some key information – details about your business offerings, contact information, keywords, etc. It's really important to be consistent as you create these listings – down to any abbreviations in your address (Street vs. St.). Your listings need to be absolutely uniform in their details. Some of these listings will require a confirmation process where you'll either need to take a phone call or receive a postcard with a confirmation code.

Submitting your business to these listing sites can take weeks to complete. Not a fun process, but again, with business you'll get faster at it, and it's really important.

Submission to Directories

Search engines are typically automated, so inclusion's pretty much guaranteed if you submit your website correctly. Directories are different. There are human editors there, and your submission will be scrutinized before it's accepted. There are directories for nearly every topic under the sun.

You can find directories relevant to your business with a Google search for: (whatever your business is) directories. This will give you a long list of directories where you can submit your site.

You'll need the same basic information you used for submitting to search engines and business listings. Again, make sure you're consistent with the information you provide in your submission.

Article Marketing
This task is a lot more interesting than directory submission! Because you're an expert in your field, writing articles is probably going to be fairly easy for you. There are guidelines you'll want to follow to make sure your articles are effective, though. With that in mind, here's a little primer on getting the most out of article marketing.

Article marketing serves two primary purposes for your business. First, it's a great way to build high-quality backlinks to your website. Remember, Google's looking for indicators that your site is an authority, that it's relevant to your keywords, that other sites respect your site enough to link to it.

If you know enough about a topic to write an article, that's a good sign. If you go to all the trouble to submit your article to respected article directories online, that's a good sign. If your article gets republished by other websites, that's a good sign. If you get a bunch of readers reading your article, that's also good.

Contrast that with spammers, who throw up a quick website, fill it with garbage text, and stuff keywords into it and you'll see why Google likes high-quality articles. There's a saying in the specialty that "content is king". If you think about it, only an expert could write an endless number of articles about their topic, and write them in a way that makes sense and provides value to their readers.

So, article marketing is a great way to make Google like your site. But it's also a good way to win human admirers, too. Think about a problem you've ever faced. If you did a Google search on that problem and landed on an article written by someone who truly understood the problem, gave helpful advice, and all along seemed credible, you'd be really glad to have found them. You'd consider them an expert and be far more willing to do business with them than some stranger who simply ran an online ad. In fact, you'd even come to the point of feeling like you knew, liked, and trusted this person – especially if they gave away valuable tips and information that helped you.

This is what we're after with your article marketing campaign.

Who Should Write Your Articles?
Either you or someone you trust to do a good job. Your articles may be the first impression someone gets of your business. They don't need to be prize-winning pieces of literature, but you certainly don't want them to be full of grammatical or logical problems.

For sure you want to either learn how to write effective articles yourself or else outsource this task to a pro. If you're concerned about getting the right information or perspective into your articles if you're not personally writing them, there's an easy solution for this.

If you're working with a ghostwriter and want to be sure they come from the right perspective as they write for you, you can provide examples of other articles you approve. It's as easy as emailing links to articles you like, or you could even set up a bookmarking account (for example, delicious.com) where you can tag articles you like and make that list available to your writer.

Another way you can guide a ghostwriter is to provide audios they can work from to create articles that are in alignment with your perspective. You can either record yourself with a voice recorder or use a recording phone line and provide the link to the audio to your writer. It's much faster and easier to speak about your topic than to write it, and in most cases you could provide enough source information for a good article in just a few minutes.

What's Involved in Article Marketing?
Whoever does the writing, there are certain guidelines you'll want to follow to do this right:

- Your articles MUST be 100% original. Google will find out if you copy someone else's writing, and this will not go well for you.
- Your article should be between 400-700 words. If it's shorter, the major article directories will reject it. If it's much longer, nobody will want to read it; you'd be better off chopping it into two separate articles.
- Your article should be written the way people speak. Never use a big word when a small word will do. Remember that people's attention span is very short online – and their willingness to 'work' to read your article is pretty much non-existent.
- Make it easy for them to read. In fact, you want to write at about a 5th-8th grade reading level for best results.

- You'll need a compelling title, a teaser (1-2 sentence summary that compels a reader to choose your article to read, even if it appears in a long list of other articles they could choose), the body of the article, and a resource box (this is a few sentences at the end of the article that features your website URL and gives some reason for a reader to click through to your site).
- Make sure you format your article in a way that encourages people to read it. No long blocks of text – short paragraphs, bullet points, and white space are important.
- Use one of your keywords for each article. The keyword should appear early in the title, in the teaser, in the first sentence, in any subheads, in your resource box, and in your anchor text in the resource box. You want to aim for about 1-2% keyword density in your article.

Writing your article is not enough. You need to submit it online to get any benefits from article marketing. We'll cover how you'll do that next.

What Is Article Submission?

There are thousands of article directories online. Some of them are huge – others are tiny. These are collections of articles on nearly any topic. Some of them accept articles on any topic – others are focused only on a single topic.

Most of them make money by having ads – in most cases they get a small payment anytime someone clicks the ads. By growing the directory and becoming known for having quality content, these sites can become very lucrative for their owners. Their business model only works if they can load up on articles people actually want to read.

These directories are frequented by people seeking information, and by website owners who want to re-publish articles rather than creating their own content. In that case, the articles are free to the website owner as long as the article is republished in its original form, complete with its resource box intact. It's a system that works well for everyone involved.

Some of these directories are automated and accept every article that's submitted. Others have stringent guidelines and human editors who must review and approve every article they publish. Google especially likes that kind of directory because there's almost no chance a garbage article will get published.

For most of these directories, you'll need to create an account for your business. Some allow you to just paste your article into a submission box – but most want you to create an account and submit that way. The better directories have a probationary period where your articles are heavily scrutinized before they're approved. With those, you'll be limited as to how many articles you can submit at a time until you've been vetted.

In a nutshell, what happens when you submit your articles to directories is that you cast a vote for your site being an authority on behalf of those directories. You create a backlink each time your article is published online, in each of those directories. Google takes notice!

The submission process isn't much fun. It's repetitive, boring, and often full of snags. You'll find it's anything but guaranteed your article will be accepted. You've got to learn and follow the guidelines for each of the major sites at least, to have a chance of having your article published. Some of the most frequent problems that could get your article rejected include:

- It's coming up as being 'duplicate content' meaning too much of your wording is too similar to something else that's been published online.
- It's too promotional. You can be promotional in blog posts on your site, but not in articles. The

editors just want valuable, useful information – not a sales pitch.
- The keyword density is too high. If your keyword appears with more than 2% frequency, some of the directories will reject your article or ask you to rewrite it.
- If you've got objectionable content, or content that otherwise violates the author's guidelines, it'll be rejected.
- If you try to include links in the body of your article, it'll be rejected. Links (usually a maximum of two) are usually acceptable in the resource box of your article – but in the better directories, they can't appear in the body.

While there are thousands of article directories out there, you can get some good results even just by submitting your article to a few of the best ones. In many cases, your article will get republished in many places because a website owner found your article in that directory. At a bare minimum, you'll want to submit your article to EzineArticles.com, currently one of the most-respected article directories out there.

How Many Articles Do You Need?
Article marketing should be a regular part of your marketing campaign. The more you do, the better – as

long as you follow the guidelines above to create high-quality articles. Ten articles a month would be enough to make a powerful impact fairly quickly. One a month would be way more than most business owners do on a regular basis. It depends on your resources.

What Should You Write About?
Whether you write for yourself or outsource this task, you'll need to come up with a list of topics to cover. Your keyword list is a great place to start. You can use your list and the topic discovery methods listed in the section on blogging to come up with some great ideas.

There are two types of articles that are proven to be a hit with readers and publishers: Top 10 lists and how-to articles. The reason the list-type article is so popular is that a reader's chances of finding valuable information that scratches their particular itch is multiplied by how many points are in the list. The how-to article is a reader favorite because it's actionable and pretty much guaranteed to feature good content.

If you check out an article directory like EzineArticles.com, you can see what kinds of articles are most read and most republished. Use what you learn to create articles that are likely to be well received like that.

Press Releases

Press releases are one of the most powerful ways to build your online presence. Google LOVES them. By nature, they're high-quality content (just the facts – no promotion), and in most cases are reviewed and approved by a human editor.

Most business owners completely ignore press releases as part of their marketing strategy because they don't think they've got news to share, they're still stuck in thinking of traditional media, and they don't know how to do a good press release.

As far as having news to share, pretty much anything going on in your business can be turned into a newsworthy event. Do a quick Google search on reasons to send a press release, and you'll find hundreds of happenings your business could use for ideas. It doesn't have to be earth-shattering news – just news.

As far as traditional media goes, the odds of your press release leading to a newspaper article, TV spot, radio interview, or anything even close to that are slim. That's not the point. The point is to get some of the highest quality backlinks available by publishing your press release online. You're not at the mercy of a journalist or print publisher who's got space restraints and needs to sell papers – publishing a press release online is much, much easier. Of course, you can submit your press releases to traditional media outlets and hope for the best – in some cases your story will get picked up. But don't focus on that.

As far as not knowing how to do a good press release, that's easy to fix, too. If you're working with an online marketing firm, they'll handle it for you. If you're not, you can outsource this task to a ghostwriter. The best ones have a simple questionnaire you can complete so they'll have all the information they need to create a great press release for you. And if you want to handle this task on your own, you can find books and courses online to learn all the particulars.

The basics you'll need to know as you write press releases for your business:

- These are news pieces. You can't have salesy language at all – just the facts.
- Make sure you cover the who, what, where, when, why, and how to get a complete story.
- You'll need to use neutral and impersonal language. This is different from your blog posts and articles, where you can be more personable. A press release shouldn't have first- or second-

person pronouns in it. The only exception is in the quote segment. You'll want to quote someone: an expert, a business representative, a customer, someone like that. This quote is the only place in the whole press release that can be slightly promotional, opinionated, or personal. It's also the only part that can include a first- or second- person pronoun.
- You'll need a strong headline that compels someone to read the release.
- Use one of your keywords per press release. It should appear in the headline, the summary, early in the first sentence, and then sprinkled throughout the release where it fits naturally.
- Follow a press release template to be sure you cover all the pieces and parts and have them in the proper order and format.

You'll need to submit your press releases to press release distribution sites in order to get any results. There are dozens that are good and free, and one that's fantastically powerful and rather pricey. That one's PRWeb.com – and you'll need to spend a small fortune per press release (just for distribution – you've got to write it) if you go that route. For many businesses, that's not an issue. For businesses that have an acute public relations problem, it's worth it. A press release distributed through that site will show nearly immediate and totally massive search engine domination.

If you're not in the middle of a crisis or don't have that much allocated for press release marketing, just do a search in Google for press release distribution sites. For some of them, you have to create an account – for others you just upload the release. Obviously the free sites will yield just a tiny fraction of the results you'd get with PRWeb.

Video Marketing
Video is one of the hottest marketing tools online today. Studies show that websites featuring videos get visitors staying longer than if there was just text on that page. Google notices how long your visitors stay, of course, so anything you can do to get them to stay longer and visit more of your pages is good.

One reason video marketing is so effective is that Google loves video – in fact it loves video so much it bought YouTube! It's always a good idea to feed Google the kind of content it loves best.

Most business owners think first of TV ad type videos – and those are great, but can be very expensive to create. There are several other types of video you could create for a fraction of the cost. Most of the video creation processes will require some software and a bit of a learning curve. Local online marketing professionals typically have this technology and know-how to create high-quality videos. Outsourcing this task may be a better use of your resources, but some business owners may want to try it on their own.

Article Videos

Once you've got articles created for your business, you could transform them into video. There are several ways to do this – one is to paste your content into a PowerPoint presentation, then record the presentation using a screen recording tool like Camtasia. For audio, you could go with nothing, music, or reading the article aloud.

Image Videos

You could also create videos that focus on graphics. Using professional stock photography and little bits of text, you can create some very visually appealing videos. There are a few software programs that make this easy and kind of fun to do. Be sure to use music and images that are approved for commercial use.

Live Action Videos
This is more like a TV ad sort of video. You'll need to have a professional video company help with this, unless you own top-notch video equipment and editing software.

What Should You Do with Your Videos?
You should include videos on your website – on the Home page and any other page that could be made more appealing and interactive by adding a video. Your blog can also include videos.

You should also create a channel on YouTube for your business. This will help your prospects and customers to stay focused on your videos rather than finding just one and then ending up watching videos from your competitors, or videos that are completely off-topic. If you have a channel for your business, all of your videos will appear to the side, and your viewers can watch your whole lineup with far less distraction.

Other than on your site, you'll need to distribute your videos just like you do with your articles and press releases. There are a number of syndication tools that help this process, but typically they're out of reach for individual business owners – only an online marketer would have enough projected usage to justify the investment in these.

You can, of course, distribute your videos on your own – it'll just take more hands-on work. Do a Google search for: video sharing sites. Other than YouTube, there are several other video distribution sites you may be able to submit to, depending on your topic and the type of video you've created. Be sure to use your keywords in the title and description of your videos.

Website traffic generation isn't the only way you can use video to increase your customers' trust, your credibility, and your profits, though. Many businesses get great results by placing TV screens or iPads on-site. They run video or educational slides featuring ways to help their customers get even better results from their products and services. This is a powerful way to show in-house educational promotions for new products and services.

Those are the primary types of marketing pieces every business needs to create and distribute online to build high-quality backlinks. In the next chapter, you'll learn how to use Google's map listings for maximum results.

Winning Your Neighborhood

Google's local listings (it's had a few different names… but it's those map listings you see when you do a Google search for a local business) is one of the most powerful tools you can use for your business – if you do it right. In fact, as many as 70% of online searches turn out to be for local businesses, products, and services. Google spotted this trend and is leveraging it big time, featuring local results at the top of search results pages.

These pages are already indexed and in most cases show up on page one. In fact, many business owners who are just learning about this tool are shocked to see their business is in the top spot – and they haven't even completed their profile yet. If you optimize your profile, you'll see your listing's effectiveness skyrocket.

Your profile will display basic information about your business. If you haven't done anything with it yet, there still may be information there – gathered from the online Yellow Pages and other directories. Just because it's there doesn't mean it's correct information – or that you can't vastly improve the results you'll get by tweaking your page. Here are the basics you need to know about maximizing the power of your Google profile page.

Provide Complete Information
Just by completing your profile, you'll make it easy for your prospective customers to get the information they need and want about your business. This boosts your odds of them becoming your customers.

Make sure you include the following:
- Hours of operation
- Brands you carry (if relevant)
- Special offers, coupons
- Photos, videos, virtual tours
- Links to your website, blog and social media profiles

Even if you don't do more than that, at least get your page claimed – or someone else may do it! It's sneaky; it's wrong; it happens all the time. Your competitor may claim your page to keep you from using it!

Once you've claimed your page, there's still a lot more you can do to turn it into a traffic-generation tool that increases your Google prominence dramatically. Here are eight tips for getting the most from your listing:

1. Help your new customers find you easily. Use the exact name and precise address to describe your business and location.
2. Make it easy for them to call you. Always use a local phone number answered by a real person.
3. Show them your site. List a link (make sure it works!) to your website. Many of your prospects will check out your site before calling you.
4. Categorize your business. Google business profile pages give you several to choose from. Be as specific as you can – if you find one with your keyword, that's even better.
5. Make your listing irresistible. You'll be able to use your keywords and your unique selling proposition in the "Description and Custom" fields for your business.

6. Let them see you. You can upload photos and videos to add even more credibility to your listing. People love to get as much info as possible about your business before calling, and this adds a bit of a personal touch and helps them feel like they know, like, and trust you.
7. Don't be shy. Publicize your positive reviews and testimonials by asking your happy customers to leave a review for your business on your Google profile page. This will help get "social proof" working in your favor – people like doing business with businesses lots of people like.
8. Make a deal. You can offer coupons and special deals to visitors to your Google business listing. This alone is a great way to pull in new customers. Be sure to have them let you know they found the deal on your Google profile page.

Follow this pattern for all of your business's online profiles. Keep them updated and optimized to get maximum impact in the search engine results. It takes a bit of time and attention to stay on top of this, but it'll pay off.

Why You Need Positive Reviews

Word of mouth advertising is the hands-down winner for most businesses – online reviews are just as powerful –

maybe more. Not only do your prospective customers take these reviews into consideration, so do the top search engines. The more positive reviews you have, the higher your business listing page will ultimately go – at least theoretically! Again, nobody knows the algorithms Google uses, and sometimes there are bizarre cases of one business with a ton of great reviews getting ranked lower than a business with no reviews, or even a couple of dings in their record.

Just think of how you search for local businesses to provide a service for you. If your roof is leaking, you'll search for a roofer in your town. Chances are, there will be several who come up on the profile section. Which one are you most likely to call?

About Getting Reviews

You might be shocked to know how many of your prospective customers go looking for reviews about your business before they'll even hit your actual website. They'll read these reviews and then decide whether to look further.

You've got to get into the routine of leveraging positive reviews. We'll get into a discussion of online reputation monitoring and marketing in a later chapter, but for now we'll just focus on getting positive reviews for your

Google listing page. You can check yours out now, if you've got a listing on Google's local pages. You'll see a star system for rating, and a couple of places where Google's practically begging your customers to leave a review.

Getting them to actually do this can be a challenge.

- Some business owners implement a subtle loyalty rewards program to encourage their customers to leave reviews. Be very careful if you go this route. Google frowns on 'buying' reviews.
- Some business owners actually pay outright for reviews. There are unscrupulous services worldwide that will sell packages of reviews super-cheap. This is a sure way to get in trouble with Google – most of the reviews are identical, vague enough to work for any type of business, and signed by the same 'users'. Google's way smarter than that, and it's just a matter of time before these businesses get caught.
- Some businesses work with a permission form to collect reviews and login information to handle posting them on behalf of their customers. Also a risky process – and not that likely to work. Would you give your login information to someone?
- One smart way some businesses tried meeting this challenge was to invest in a mobile device or iPad

they could use at their location to have happy customers leave a review on the spot. While it was a good solution while it worked, now, multiple reviews from the same device will be automatically discarded by the review sites. While this method in and of itself does not work, by using a proprietary system we developed, it is possible for this method to work again.
- You could try asking any smartphone users to leave their reviews while they're there. You'd need to help by providing an information sheet with suggestions for how to write an effective review.

Those are some ways business owners have tried to get reviews on their own – none particularly effective. Don't worry, though, in just a little while you'll learn how you can not only get great reviews, but also leverage them to use as a powerful marketing tool that propels you past your competitors and leaves them wondering what happened.

If you ignore crafting a powerful local online presence, you run the risk of making it hard for people to find your business – even if they do know your business name. You'll also leave a bad impression with your prospects because having an incomplete profile makes it look like maybe your business is out of business.

There are only so many spots in the business listings map section – typically no more than seven will appear on the first page. Beyond that and someone would have to click a little link that tells Google to show more results on the map. There is no way to pay for a higher organic placement.

You want to be sure your business is showing up on that map. Especially in larger towns and cities, it's important for your prospects to be able to gauge how close you are to their location – and to determine that yours is the nearest, best choice for them. The map makes that possible instantly. While you may lose some prospects who decide you're too far away, chances are you'd have lost them anyway once they figured out where you're located. For others who are close-by, showing up on the map close to them may be the final tipping point to steer them your way.

No denying it – there are a lot of directories and business profiles out there to manage. The task can seem overwhelming because you've already got so much on your plate. This may be a good task to hand off to an online marketing expert so you can just focus on doing what you need to do to keep your business running.

In the next chapter, we'll dive into online reputation monitoring – even from this quick overview of Google's local listing service, you can see that never before has it been more important to know what people are saying about your business online.

Protecting Your Flank

With the Internet's power, it's never been more important to know what people are saying about you and your business. Someone can leave negative reviews about your business in forums, blogs, articles, press releases, websites or Google's local listings, and do major damage to your business before you even know what happened.

Take a guess what happens when a prospective customer reads negative reviews about your business – especially if they're prominently displayed at the top of Google's results... Click! They go to your competitor's site instead.

The one with the good reviews.

You can't ignore what's being said about your business. It will either help you or hurt you. Either way, you've got to know so you can help yourself.

What Is Online Reputation Monitoring?
Online reputation monitoring helps to monitor and guard your online presence. It makes it possible for you to know right away when people say anything – good or bad – about your business. That makes it possible to do damage control if it's bad, or leverage stellar reviews.

Horror stories abound about businesses that were targeted by irate customers or even malicious competitors who used the Internet to pretty nearly destroy businesses they didn't like. It's unethical, but not unheard of for people like this to build entire websites dedicated to slamming a business they decided to target. Sometimes they'll even go to great expense to publicize their discontent. In some cases, they even hijack an unclaimed Google business listing page to wreak havoc. That's bad enough, but if you don't even know it's happening, you have no chance of protecting yourself.

The Best Defense Is a Strong Offense
Reputation marketing is more than simply tracking and monitoring your online reputation. It is positioning your

business as the market leader with a five-star reputation in front of thousands of buyers.

The goal is to build a solid foundation of hundreds of five-star reviews, which translates into getting your phone ringing off the hook. The idea is to leverage that five-star reputation and use it to generate new business. Once the five-star review count is where it needs to be, it then becomes a matter of using that powerful sales tool to leverage new customers through your front door. Amass enough of these stellar reviews, and your competitors will have no chance of catching up to you.

You may run into marketing companies that tell you they will monitor your online reputation. This is fine as far as it goes, but the problem is it doesn't go far enough.

It's a given that someone should be monitoring your online reputation on an ongoing 24-7-365 basis.

Unfortunately, this alone will not get your phone ringing and door swinging. Simply monitoring your reputation will not make that happen.

How More Money Changes Hands More Often

You need to take it to the next level. You need to take the information you gather in the monitoring phase and use it to make improvements where necessary in your online reputation. It's important to remember that the goal of this entire process is to create that all-important five-star reputation.

Implement Reputation-Based Marketing Tactics

After you've gathered information in the monitoring phase, you will need to implement reputation marketing tactics specifically designed to build a five-star reputation. This in turn will catapult your business into a leadership position within the marketplace.

Once you have established yourself as a market leader, you will begin to generate presold and prequalified customers, who turn out in droves at your company.

If you find that you have recently received a series of negative reviews, you need to learn how to use that knowledge to turn things around. The goal is to truly understand your current online reputation and know what you need to do to move it in the right direction. A clear view of your current status is the first step toward getting your reputation turned around.

Your Online Reputation Becomes a Profit Center

Thanks to the latest trends in Internet-listing patterns, your company's online reputation has risen to a position of critical importance to your business. A couple of factors have come together to create the perfect storm for making – or breaking – your company.

First of all, the emergence of online customer reviews has created an environment in which those reviews form the basis for your company's online reputation. These reviews and business reputations are followed closely by prospective customers checking companies out on the Internet.

Meaning if you have a bad online reputation, your business will be adversely impacted. For example, if you've got seven online reviews and five of them are negative, you have a terrible online reputation.

On the other hand, if you have ten online reviews and all ten are five-star reviews, you are now on your way toward becoming the leader in your marketplace, and should start enjoying a steady flow of prequalified, presold customers streaming through your door.

The goal of all of this is to turn your business into a market leader. This is where the payoff comes in for working hard and generating those powerful five-star reviews. Once that happens, you will start to receive a steady flow of presold customers calling you and coming through your front door.

The Question Is, How Do You Make That Happen?
We have developed techniques to help you build a positive online reputation. It's not as difficult as you might think. The first step is to use our techniques to start generating five-star online reviews for your company. We have developed a series of tools to help us create those top reviews. Then, after generating your first fifty five-star reviews, the process kicks into overdrive to accumulate hundreds of these stellar reviews, and you'll see your business firmly planted into a leadership position within your market.

Studies have shown that not only do people trust online reviews as much as they trust their family and friends, but they also use those reviews to make a decision about your company.

If you have poor online reviews they will avoid you like the plague, but if you have fifty five-star reviews, people will trust you more than your competitor. Get hundreds of these glowing reviews, and they'll consider you the leader in your market and will trust you totally. They will, in fact, be presold on you.

What Does This Mean For Your Company?

Once you have used online reviews to create a market leadership position for your company, people will begin calling your business or coming through your front door already sold on you.

Thanks to the fact that most people trust online reviews as much as they trust the opinions of their friends and family, they will be prequalified, presold and ready to buy. When this occurs your business will reach a tipping point, and your reputation will suddenly become the true profit center for your company.

Drastic Measures

If you find yourself in the situation of needing to bury unjustified bad press, you enter into reputation repair mode. One of the fastest ways to bury bad search engine results is to displace them with positive ones that the search engines trust. There's no faster way to achieve that than to invest in a press release with PRWeb. It's costly, of course, but in some cases a press release distributed through that service will show up fairly quickly and dominate pages of search engine results. It's not a permanent fix, because as the press release ages, it becomes less powerful – but it will give you time to create other online content to help your cause.

The Hedge

OK, remember how search engines work? You type in a search term and get a list of results. Nobody's likely to go past page one unless they're really motivated to do thorough research. One way you can build a hedge of protection for yourself online is to own your own name search results. If you can lock up the whole first page or two of search results for your name and your business name, you'll make it harder for someone to blast you online.

You build the hedge first of all by making sure you own domains featuring your name and your business name. While the variations here are endless, with .com, .net, .info, .tv, .co, .org, etc., you may want to invest in several for added protection. This can be gradual. What you're doing is preventing someone else from buying a domain featuring your name.

Reputation protection is another reason to be sure you've claimed the Google local listing for your business.

You also want to be sure you create content (articles, press releases, and videos) that use your name or your business name as a keyword. They will show up and take up valuable real estate on that front page of Google, making it more challenging for someone with malicious intent to break into those top spots.

The key to online reputation monitoring, management, and repair, if it comes to that, is having a system that lets you stay vigilant in protecting yourself. It's not a task most business owners have on their radar – or know how to do efficiently, but it's important.

In the next chapter, you'll discover one of the best ways to stay in contact with your customers while helping your business to grow exponentially.

Winning On the Go

If your customer base is anything like the majority of the population, you can pretty much rely on one fact: they are completely addicted to their mobile devices. This presents a great marketing opportunity and another way your marketing can crash and burn – all in the same little gadget. You've probably heard of mobile marketing. There are a couple of meanings for that term, and we'll cover them both.

The first 'mobile marketing' is text messaging, or SMS for short. With mobile text messaging, you've got a powerful way of reaching your customers and prospective customers anytime you like. It's almost a guarantee... if you get a text message, you'll read it. Right now there's no other effective way of getting your customers to pay attention to you, especially if you make it worth their while to read your texts and take action.

Mobile marketing is one of the most effective ways you can communicate with your customers today. It won't stay that way forever, because technology is always bringing the next new thing – but for right now (and probably the next few years) this is a tool you need to consider for your business.

Here's why:
- More than 90% of adults in the U.S. own a mobile phone.
- More than 95% of all text messages get opened.
- More than 90% of those messages get opened within less than an hour.

Print, email, and other forms of advertising and promotion don't come anywhere close to the reach of mobile marketing. People just don't pay attention to any other form of communication as much as they do to texts.

You'll need to keep your messages brief so they don't get cut off. You'll also need to experiment a bit to see how frequently your customers want to hear from you. Once a week is acceptable to most customers – but what's appropriate for your communications depends on what type of business you have.

How Do You Do This?

You will need to have access to a text message marketing service for this to be manageable. It's not really a tactic you can do on your own without a messaging platform; unless you don't mind sending out just ten messages or so at a time to your entire interested customer base, gathering their mobile numbers and entering them into your phone manually, and being sure to delete any who ask to be removed from your list.

A good platform will allow for your customers to sign themselves up to receive your messages, then let you send them all at once. Typically the customer sign-up process involves posting a sign at your business offering your customers a deal for registering on the spot. They'll text a certain message to that platform in order to register – and then you'll have their mobile number and permission to send them special promotions until they ask you to stop. If that happens and you're using a mobile platform, they'll be removed from the list automatically.

This is one of those marketing methods that's worth trying out – even if you personally hate the idea of getting promotional messages on your phone. If you make it worth your customers' while to get these messages, they will like getting them. They can always unsubscribe if they get tired of hearing from you; and there are ways to make sure that doesn't happen. If you offer something of value (information, discounts, or freebies) in every text you send, your customers will read your messages almost every time.

Text messaging may not be appropriate for every business – although the applications for different business types are growing all the time. But it's worth taking a look at to see whether it'll work for yours.

The "Other" Mobile Marketing
When you hear marketers talking about mobile marketing, they may be talking about text messaging – or they might be talking about mobile-responsive websites, which function as in-pocket sales tools. It won't take long to figure out which they mean if you listen for a little while.

What Is a Mobile-Responsive Website?
The percentage of searches people do online on their mobile devices rather than on a laptop or desktop computer is skyrocketing. We're a society that's always on the go, so this makes sense. Many predict the number of

searches done on mobile devices will soon greatly outnumber searches on home computers. This means you need to know how to make your business accessible online for your customers and prospects who search for you on the fly.

You're out running errands, traveling, sitting in a meeting, waiting for your kids, or any of a million other scenarios where you're away from home – and you need to find a business that offers a certain procedure or service. Do you wait until you're home to search online for it? Not if you have a smartphone or other web-enabled device. Your customers and prospects are the same – they may be looking for you online using their mobile devices.

This is great news – if your site is mobile-responsive. Mobile sites load quickly and are easy to navigate even on the tiniest of touch screens. You know from your own experience searching online using your mobile – if a site won't load quickly enough, you move onto the next site. If the navigation on a site is complicated and slow, or requires you to complete boxes with your information, you'll bounce to a site that's easier to use.

In addition to making your navigation easy and intuitive, you need to pay attention to the priority of information you're providing. Because your mobile searchers are usually in a hurry, it's even more important that what they find on your site first meets their needs and grabs their attention so they'll stay on your site long enough to determine that your business is exactly what they need.

Does Your Site Work on Mobiles? Really?

It gets a little technical here, but to make sure your site works properly on a mobile, you'll need to make sure it's coded correctly. In some cases, all you need to do is install a plug-in that automatically determines whether a visitor is using a mobile device or regular computer to get to your site, then adjusts how the site performs. If your site was built using a platform that doesn't work with plug-ins, the coding involved is a bit more complicated and not something you'd want to try to do on your own.

No matter who built your site, and how they built it, you can check your site's performance on your own phone – then ask your friends, family, and employees to check on their mobiles as well so you can see how it shows up on different devices.

Ever See a QR Code?

You probably have – and may not have known what you were seeing. QR codes (or Quick Response codes) are a handy marketing tool that works with mobile devices. They're little square graphics you can scan with your smartphone to get a deal or some other kind of special or information. They were originally used for storing information about car parts – but are now used for marketing.

QR codes appear in newspapers, drive-by signs, in email marketing, text messages, and posters. Some businesses even have a QR code printed on the backs of their business or appointment cards. The technology allows marketers to collect and store valuable information about your customers' interests and preferences and to run analyses that will prove useful for your marketing campaigns.

Contests and coupons are some of the most successful uses of QR codes. Uses that are engaging and valuable are most likely to get your customers sharing them with their contacts, the ideal outcome.

Getting a QR code made for your business is a bit involved, but you can do it yourself with some research and technical skills. If you're working with an online marketing firm, they'll be able to help you with this as well as helping you track the performance of your codes.

You may also want to look into getting a mobile app developed for your business. Apps take mobile marketing to a whole new level by allowing customers to buy by phone, make appointments, complete forms, set up mobile bill pay, interact with you on social media, and even refer their friends and neighbors to your business. With a push notifications feature, you can alert your customers to special promotions and remind them of scheduled appointments as well. Many businesses find their mobile app helps to decrease wasted appointment slots, as they can easily fill openings quickly.

In the next chapter, we'll take a closer look at email marketing. Is this a strategy that still works? Should your business use it?

Messages that Conquer

It used to be that email marketing was THE surefire way to build a list of prospects and customers, stay in touch with them, and market to them. Now some marketers are finding that people's physical mail boxes are more fruitful ground for marketing than their email inboxes. Is email marketing still a good use of your resources? And if so, how can you get the best possible results?

You can blame it all on overload.

Way, way back in the day, getting an email was kind of exciting. The novelty wore off a long time ago, and now most people consider their email boxes a necessary evil, a mix of messages we can't wait to read and those we'd just as soon delete without ever opening. The joke now is that your email box will still be full after you die, so don't even bother trying to empty it.

If you consider the messages your spam filter ensures you never even see, you probably get hit with literally hundreds of emails every single day. How many do you open, read, and take action on?

If you subscribed to them and wanted the information, probably quite a few.

Even with its drop in effectiveness, email marketing remains an affordable tool that can get you good results if you do it right.

If you're going to use email marketing – and it's still a valuable tool for most businesses – you have to figure out how to do it so your messages get read and acted on rather than just deleted or marked as spam.

First, yes, most likely your business needs to be doing email marketing. We covered this a bit earlier, but the primary reason is that building a list of people who want to hear from you means building a valuable asset. People who find your website and are interested in what you offer, but for whatever reason don't buy right away will be lost to you forever unless they join your list, giving you permission to contact them.

Even with its drop in effectiveness, email marketing remains an affordable tool that can get you good results if you do it right. The biggest reason it still works is that the people who subscribe to your list are at least somewhat interested in what you offer.

There's a fine line between effective email marketing and spam, though. If you email too often, or don't give your readers a valuable reason to read, you'll annoy them and instead of them being eager to learn more or do business with you, you'll leave them wanting nothing to do with you.

Again with the fine line, but if you email too infrequently, you'll have the opposite problem. People who were once interested in your business will forget who you are or why they were interested in the first place.

Balance is important. You need to have balance in your frequency of emailing and the mix of promotional and informational content. If every message you send is an advertisement, your readers will unsubscribe in droves. A good mix some marketers find is about 25% promotional and 75% informational.

Now, on to some particulars about how to do this right.

Make the Subject Line Count.
Mess this up, and nobody will read your emails. The subject line is a lot like the headline on a newspaper. It needs to be clear and catchy, but not hype-filled or misleading. Walk this fine line or risk aggravating your readers.

Avoid Long, Wordy Messages.
People are too busy to read paragraph after endless paragraph. Write your emails so they're easy to skim, scan, and scroll through. Subheads and bullets help with this.

Include a Call to Action.
Decide what you want your reader to do next. Do you want them to buy something? Click something? Download something? Call you? Come into your location? They won't automatically do it; you have to tell them, and give them a reason to do it. Don't give them a long list of actions to take – make it simple... ask them to do ONE thing.

Identify Yourself.
We read left to right – and that holds true in our email boxes as well. There are a lot of decisions being made in a

fraction of a second when someone gets your email. We tend to open emails only if we recognize the sender and trust that reading their message will be worth our time and attention. The "from" field of an email may be even more important than the subject line now – especially for your existing customers.

Be sure to include your contact information in plain sight within your email message as well. Include: phone numbers, website address, and your business's physical address.

Get Someone Else to Write for You.
Writing may not be your strength – or the best use of your time. Many business owners hire ghostwriters to create their email messages for them. It's worth the investment to have well-written, professional emails reaching your customers and prospects.

Edit, Proofread and Do It Again.
If you decide to write your own messages, remember that spelling errors and incorrect grammar can land your messages right in the trash bin. Make sure your content is perfect and professional.

There's a lot that goes into a successful email marketing strategy – and you can learn more by taking a course or reading up on the topic online. Many businesses decide to hand off this task to a marketing partner rather than spending the time and energy involved in doing it effectively.

In the next chapter, you'll learn how to tap into the world of social media profitably for your business.

Wooing the Crowd

Love them or hate them, the worlds of Facebook, Twitter, LinkedIn, Google+, Instagram, Pinterest and the whole rest of the social side of the Internet represent money in the bank for the business that uses them right.

Ignore social media at your own peril – use it wrong and you may as well throw money through a shredder; but do it right, and you'll position your business in a sweet spot where you can connect with your prospects and turn them into lifelong customers who can't stop raving about your products and services.

Not sure social media's all it's cracked up to be for local marketing? Google and Bing have both revealed they weigh social media into their local search results. They don't reveal anything about how this information figures into their algorithms of course, but just knowing they're looking makes it worthwhile to work with a social media campaign if you want to dominate the search engines for your market. Could mean the difference between a top ranking and slipping onto page two or lower.

Why Should You Bother?
What works is always changing. Traditional methods of marketing lose their effectiveness, or come back into power – you never know what'll happen next, what will be the next best way to reach your target market. Right now, social media is one of the most affordable and profitable ways to get new customers into your business. These prospects are online – and social media is one of the easiest ways to reach them right there.

Social media is the closest relative to word-of-mouth advertising available to you as someone who sells what they need. It's a great way to get near-instant credibility, even loyalty, with current customers while you attract new ones. People flock to these sites to get information and to connect with others – and they don't just do it now and then; most people check into their accounts multiple times a day.

Create a social media plan, build an effective presence on these sites, post relevant content, and see how easy it is to cement your position as an expert in your specialty. While branding is just part of the picture, you'll find it's easy to subtly create brand awareness among your followers and friends online. This is because with these sites, you can relate to your ideal customers meaningfully and regularly. By paying attention to their updates, you can also gather valuable market research pretty easily.

Lots of businesses wonder how they'll know whether their social media campaigns are actually working. The best way to measure your results is to gauge how much people interact with your profiles – and ultimately, of course, whether you see an uptick in new customers coming into your business. Do they "like" and "share" and "follow" and re-post your comments and updates? Do they post positive reviews and testimonials on your page? Link to your profile from theirs?

Setting Up Your Profiles

You'll want to set up a business profile – even if you have a personal profile – on Facebook and Twitter at a minimum. LinkedIn, Google+, Instagram, and Pinterest may be helpful to you as well. Make sure your profile is as complete as possible and that you've used your keywords where appropriate.

Don't believe for a minute that any one social media site is enough – no matter how much you like or hate a particular site, there are millions of users who prefer one or the other and use it regularly. Ignoring either could mean leaving lots of business on the table. You need to be on the sites your customers and prospects use.

Privacy is not your friend on these sites when it comes to marketing your business. While you might want your personal profile to be accessible only to people you know, your business profile needs to be public. This will help your search engine ranking, where a private page will do nothing to help you move up in the search results.

The Name of the Game Is Being Liked… A Lot
Liked, followed, connected – it all comes down to people finding value in being associated with you in social media. The more popular your business is among the users of these sites, the wider your reach.

Getting people to connect with you can take some finesse. Don't beg people to "like" or "follow" you on social media – give them a reason to want to do it. Discounts on your products or services, free gifts, and valuable information remain prime incentives.

Make it easy for people on your mobile marketing or email marketing list to connect with you via social media. Include your Twitter, Facebook, and LinkedIn info and a special offer for those who connect there. This is a great way to put your prior marketing efforts to use another way.

Consider using Facebook advertising to build your fan base. If you do it right, it's cost-effective and you can target your prospects very narrowly. You can make it so your ad only shows up for users from certain demographics, geographical areas, or with specific interests.

Who Should You Hang Out With?

Be on the lookout for businesses that are complimentary to yours, for example, Chiropractors, targeting the same ideal customer you're looking for – then see how you could connect with these business owners and help them. If you work together, you can find ways to grow both businesses as you better serve your customer base.

Bing in particular seems to pay attention to your fans and followers as well as who you're following. This makes it worthwhile to seek out prominent businesses with lots of followers and connect with them.

What Should You Post?

Stay relevant and fresh. Put some thought into what you post – don't just do the same old thing all the time. You can do some quick research to find out what people are interested in related to your products and services – then write your updates from your perspective on these popular topics.

Preserve your positioning as an expert by guarding your content. If it's junk, don't post it. If it's going to throw your business's professional image into question, don't post it. Never post if you don't have anything valuable to post. There's always something you can post that will add value to your followers – even if it takes a little bit of digging and thinking to come up with it.

You can leverage your work by linking your social media sites, or at least using the same posts and updates across the board among the sites. Chances are you'll have different followers on each of the social media sites – at least in part. Beyond that, both Google and Bing say links posted on both Facebook and Twitter weigh into their algorithms.

Your competitors are using social media – that's pretty much guaranteed. No matter how you feel about these sites, you can't afford not to use them. It can seem overwhelming at first – and it is a big task to stay on top of your social media campaign. But it will pay off for you in building more and better connections online with your prospects and existing customers if you'll dedicate the resources you need to do it right.

Seems like a lot of tasks to juggle, doesn't it? In the next chapter, you'll learn how to keep all of this online marketing going throughout the year without letting anything slip through the cracks.

Map Out Your Plan

It all comes back to having a plan. Marketing your business effectively online won't just happen. It's a big job, one you can't just leave to chance or do when you get around to it.

There's no way you'll be able to stay on top of all the tasks involved in online marketing without a marketing calendar. You've got enough to do just running your business without trying to save space in your brain for remembering when you'll do what for promotion. Before you know it, holidays creep up on you and marketing opportunities are lost because you somehow didn't see them coming or just didn't have the resources needed to reach out to your prospects and customers.

Every one of the tactics and strategies in this book needs to be done on a regular basis for best results. There's just no getting around it – either you need to do this for your business, or you need to outsource this battery of tasks so it actually gets done, running like clockwork.

Here's how the professionals handle it: they use a marketing calendar. This could be as simple as creating a spreadsheet with an area for each month and each tactic, then a plan to follow. A marketing calendar makes it easy to keep track of what's coming next, what's actually been done, how much it cost, and how it worked for your business.

Using a marketing calendar also makes it easy to capitalize on events and holidays throughout the year. You can do a quick search online to find a list of holidays – everything from the usual holidays you already know about to some that are strange, funny, creative, controversial, or obscure. Every single month there's something you could use to tie into your business, connect with your prospects and customers, and create revenue.

It can take a while to find the ideal marketing mix. How many articles, press releases, videos, and blog posts do you need each month? How many social media updates per week? What should you text or email to your customers?

But rather than waiting until you magically guess correctly at the answers to these questions for your business, you'll do better to get started. The sweet spot for your particular business may take some time to discover – but you won't find it by speculating. And most likely it won't stay the same for long. As new tactics arise, you'll need to work out how to incorporate them into your online marketing plan, too.

Having a marketing calendar spreadsheet makes it easy to track your results so you can do more of what's working best for you, and begin to understand what might be going wrong on tactics that aren't producing the results you want. You'll have to really keep your eye on all of this if you're doing it yourself so that you don't waste even a minute of your very limited time. Even if you end up working with an online marketing firm, you'll want to keep tabs on your results.

Some metrics you'll find important to look at monthly at a minimum:

- Website traffic. What really counts is unique visitors. You'll find a lot of other counts, like hits

and pages, but what you really care most about is how many different people visit your site.
- Website dominance. An online marketer has tools that report how your site is ranking for a whole host of keywords, but you can do some poking around in Google to see how you're doing for some of your top keywords. Just do a search using your keywords and see where you come up.
- How are your new customers finding you? Make it a practice to ask them so you'll know which strategies are paying off best for you.

Keep an eye on your return on marketing investment. Very few business owners have any idea how much it costs them to acquire a new customer, or even how much that new customer will be worth to them in the coming year. These are valuable figures to know because they will help you make better decisions about your marketing. Almost every business owner has run a marketing campaign that went into the red – but to do it again and again because you're not aware of your results is a sure way to end up losing hard-earned revenue.

In the end, marketing your business online is a huge job. It's not one you can ignore. The Internet's not going anywhere anytime soon. Overwhelming? Possibly. But it's also an opportunity to reach your market like you've never had before. Compared with traditional forms of advertising, you can reach exponentially more prospects for the same money. It's all about having – and following – a solid plan.

Hopefully this little book has given you a much clearer understanding of what you need to do to promote your business effectively. If you decide you'd like some assistance so you can focus on running your business instead of all the tasks involved in marketing it, let me know. We can take a close look at how your business is doing now, what's needed to improve your visibility, and how we can reach your goals together.

Glossary

Above the Fold
Just like on a newspaper at a newsstand, you can only see part without flipping the paper over. On a website, this is the part that's visible without scrolling.

Affiliate
Someone who promotes your products and services and gets paid based on results.

Algorithm
How search engines create a list of search results based on the search term. Algorithms change regularly to yield better search results.

ALT Text
Coding that tells the search engines about images and other non-textual elements that can't be displayed.

Analytics
Graphs and charts that provide information on your website's traffic and the source and behavior of your site's visitors.

Anchor Text
Words, phrases, or images that are 'clickable' – when you click, you are taken to another part of the website or elsewhere on the Internet.

B2B
Business to Business marketing

B2C
Business to Consumer marketing

Backlinks
Links coming into your website from another place online. Backlinks help with SEO because some algorithms calculate the quantity and quality of backlinks when determining search engine result ranking.

Below the Fold
Any part of a webpage you have to scroll down to see.

Black Hat SEO
Search engine optimization that uses unethical methods.

Blog
An online journal or article page that is updated frequently, usually allows comments.

Bots
Short for the robots (also called spiders) that scan the Internet for search engines.

Bounce
When a visitor reaches your website and leaves it quickly without visiting any other pages on your site.

Bounce Rate
The percentage of your site visitors that bounce.

Browser
An application that enables you to access and navigate the Internet.

Code
Information written in any of several computer languages.

Competing Pages

The total of webpages that are focused on a single keyword.

Conversion Rate

The percentage of how many clicks to your site generate a sale or a lead.

Crawl

An automated process where search engine algorithms gather information about websites.

Deep Linking

Linking to a page on your website other than your Home Page.

Description Tag

An HTML (code) tag that provides a description of the page for search engine listings.

Directory

An index of websites, usually created by human editors. Usually require editorial approval for inclusion.

Directory Optimization

Writing a directory submission in a way that makes it most relevant for search engines to increase the chances of the site coming up when someone searches with your keywords.

Domain
A text Internet address ending in a dot and three letters (i.e. .com, .net., .org, etc.). In countries outside the U.S. domain names end with a two letter country code.

Duplicate Content
Webpages that have the same content – can be on a single website or on different websites.

Ecommerce
Buying and selling products and services online.

Flame
Comments or messages posted with the intention of being rude or abusive.

Geo Targeting
Adding geographical information to marketing campaigns to make the marketing pieces more likely to appear to searchers in that location.

Google Dance
Each time Google changes its algorithms, Internet marketers scramble to understand the impact of that

change and then make any adjustments needed to their online marketing.

Google Sandbox
For various reasons – from having a brand new site to employing Black Hat SEO tactics – sometimes Google essentially shuns a website, and it basically disappears from search engine results.

Google Smack
Getting your site put into the Google Sandbox.

Google Update
An adjustment in Google's search algorithm, usually resulting in Google Smacks. Notable Updates of the recent past include the Panda and Penguin.

Googlebot
See bot.

Hidden Text
Text added to a webpage that is the same color as the page's background, making it invisible to humans. Search engines can read the text. This is a Black Hat SEO tactic.

Home Page
The main page of a website, its main point of entry.

Hyperlink
A bit of text or an image you can click on a webpage that takes you somewhere else, either on that page or to another page or another website.

Inbound Link
Any link that comes into your site from another website.

Keyword
What someone types in when they search for information online. Can be a single word or a phrase.

Keyword Density
How many times a keyword appears on a page for every 100 words.

Keyword Research
Research done to determine how people are searching online for the information, products, and services you offer.

Keyword Stuffing (or Keyword Spam)
Trying to include too many repetitions of a keyword in an article or website content in an effort to trick search engines into giving higher importance to the website. This is a Black Hat SEO tactic.

Keywords Tag

A list of relevant keywords for a website, entered into the coding of the site. Early on, the search engines paid attention to the keywords tag – now most ignore it completely, as its abuse was an easy Black Hat SEO tactic.

Landing Page

The page on a website where you land after clicking through a link on another website – either from an affiliate's page, an article, press release, or video. It is designed to get a visitor to take action.

Link Building

An SEO business with the goal of boosting a website's traffic and improving its ranking in the search engines. Links can be created with articles, press releases, videos, blog posts, etc.

Link Checker

An automated tool that helps identify broken hyperlinks on a website.

Link Popularity

How many sites link to your site, and how well-respected by the search engines those sites are.

List
An email marketing list comprised of site visitors who provided their name and email address, willingly giving you permission to market to and contact them.

Long Tail
Keyword phrases 2-5 words long. They get fewer searchers, but they are more targeted and often yield better conversion rates.

Manual Submission
Building backlinks by hand rather than by using an automated tool.

Meta Tags
Bits of code that provide information to search engines about a website. They include Title Tags, Description Tags, and Keyword Tags.

Navigation
How you move from page to page in a website.

Organic Search Listings
Listings in a search engine that are not sponsored, or purchased, as an advertisement.

Outbound Link
A link that leads to a website that's not your site.

Page Rank
Search engines use algorithms to determine the relevance of a website, then list them in order of relevance.

Podcasts
Audios and videos that can be distributed online, downloaded, and played on a personal computer or mobile device.

PPC (Pay Per Click)
Paid placement in a search engine. Your ads only show up when someone enters the keywords you bid on for your ad. You only pay when someone clicks your ad.

Reciprocal Links
Links exchanged between website owners.

RSS (Real Simple Syndication)
A way to syndicate your blog content online so it reaches subscribers automatically every time you update the content.

Search Engine
A program that scours the Internet in the attempt to match searches and web pages.

SEO (Search Engine Optimization)
Working on a website to make sure it is found easily by people using targeted keywords to search for information, products, and services online.

Search Engine Submission
Submitting URLs to search engines to make the engine aware of their existence.

SERP (Search Engine Results Page)
The results you see after doing a search in a search engine. The SERP includes sponsored ads and organic search listings in a list.

Social Media
Various websites that feature user-contributed content, including social networking sites, forums, blogs, video sharing sites, and more.

Title Tag
An HTML tag coded to create the text that shows up in the top line of a browser when you visit a website. Also

used by search engines to help them provide relevant search results.

Top Ten

The top ten websites appearing in the organic search listings on a SERP.

Unique Visitor

An actual, real visitor to your website. Unique visitor stats don't include bots or repeat visitors, so this is an important statistic to measure.

URL

The Internet location of a webpage. Follows the format http://www.domain.com (or other domain endings).

Web Directory

An organized, categorized listing of websites, sometimes centered around a specific topic.

About the Author

Tom Carolan is an expert in the growing field of online marketing for local businesses, and the author of *Goliath Is Falling!* His first business endeavor, Carolans Property Services, a company he founded in London, was nominated for "The Best Small Business of the Year Award" from the Prince of Wales Business Trust in December 1993. That business delivered an astounding 1000% return on investment for its venture capital partners. In the US, Tom's proven his insurance marketing expertise in over 13 years at Parasol Leads. As President and CEO, he led the company to the "Best Leads Quality in America" award from the LeadsCouncil in January 2014. In fact since 2007, Parasol Leads has maintained an A+ Rating for Customer Satisfaction from the Better Business Bureau each and every year. Always evolving, Tom continues to raise the bar in customer expectations as he drives their success into the online marketing world.

Tom's insatiable hunger for understanding has resulted in a diversified education and the ability to grasp what's most important to learn about any strategy, tactic, or tool useful for marketing. His commitment to serving others shows up in his long list of recommendations from clients and colleagues alike.

Tom's clients benefit from his unrivaled connections, integrity, expertise, and effectiveness. His passion is helping his clients compete better online so they can grow their businesses, benefitting their employees, clients, vendors, networking partners, and communities alike.

Be sure to request your complimentary consultation, an overview of your current online marketing strategy from an unbiased professional. Tom will discuss with you what you're doing well on your site, what elements could use improvement, and some suggestions you can use to get better results.

You can connect with Tom on LinkedIn here:

By phone: 805-474-8111

On LinkedIn: www.linkedin.com/in/tomacarolan

www.ingramcontent.com/pod-product-compliance
Lightning Source LLC
Chambersburg PA
CBHW051531170526
45165CB00002B/697